LAGONDA
HERITAGE

D1439568

LAGONDA HERITAGE

Richard Bird

First published in Great Britain in 1994 by Osprey, an imprint of Reed Consumer Books Limited, Michelin House, 81 Fulham Road, London SW3 6RB and Auckland, Melbourne, Singapore and Toronto

ISBN 185532 363 X

Project Editor Shaun Barrington
Editor Jim Walton
Page Design by Paul Kime/Ward Peacock Partnership
Printed in Hong Kong

Front cover
Geoff Seaton's well known 1930 3 litre is regarded by many Lagonda owners as the best one surviving. The 3 litre was the last model to have a Lagonda-designed engine, subsequent cars incorporating engines from outside manufacturers until the W. O. Bentley V12 which was specially designed for Lagonda and made its appearance in 1937. Geoff Seaton is pretty famous himself, as a Lagonda author

Back cover
The Roy Eccles Brooklands car. Although this supercharged special is a Rapier, its Lagonda heritage lurks beneath the skin

Half title page
Douglas Brown's 1935 M45 Tourer; see page 72

Title page
Nick Channing's 1939 V12 Tourer; see page 114. Surprisingly, the wonderful metallic paint was the original colour

Right
Barry Jones' 3 Litre Low Chassis; see page 60. Barry Jones has been known to refer to the car – as do other 3 litre owners – as the 'Lagonda Lagonda'. That is, the last one with the Lagonda-designed engine

For a catalogue of all books published by Osprey Automotive please write to:

The Marketing Department, Reed Consumer Books, 1st Floor, Michelin House, 81 Fulham Road, London SW3 6RB

Introduction

Lagonda's founder, Wilbur Gunn, was born in Springfield , Ohio in 1859. Although he was an accomplished musician who originally came to England as an opera singer, it is for his engineering, not his arias, that he is remembered today. Gunn's contribution to automotive history began in 1898, when, having already built a fast steam yacht called Giralda that won races on the Thames, he started to make motorbikes in his greenhouse in Staines. The same greenhouse eventually became the Lagonda factory, Lagonda being the Shawnee Indian word for what is now Buck Creek in Gunn's native Springfield.

The motorbikes were very highly regarded, and represented Britain in the International Cup. Then, in 1904, Gunn was joined by A. H. Cranmer, and the two men progressed to three-wheeled cars. Within a year, these had been further developed, and boasted twin-cylinder, water-cooled engines of around 1200cc. Later, wheel steering was also added. It is thought that about seventy of these tri-cars were built, of which only three are still in existence. Sadly, as far as we know, no Lagonda motorbike has survived — one was around in 1930, but has since disappeared. After Gunn's death in 1920 at the age of 61, Cranmer remained Technical Director of Lagonda until his retirement in 1935.

Meanwhile, following the success of his three-wheelers, Gunn designed a 10hp car, mostly using the parts, including the engine, from the last tri-car model. He made only a few, however, before going on to develop larger cars — one using a Coventry-Simplex and JAP carburettor, another, even bigger and with heavier axles, using a Polyroe carburettor and electric lighting. This 16/18 hp vehicle continued to use parallel trailing links to locate it. Then, about 1910, a 30hp engine appeared, with six cylinders in pairs and a removable hard top as an option. The next innovation was the Light Car...

Contents

The Light Car

BK 2371 c.1913 11.1 two-seater Coupé c.1913

Steve Lawrence's 11.1 is a charming example of the first Light Car that Wilbur Gunn produced. So called because of its small size, low running costs and cheap price the Light Car nevertheless retained the reliability of the bigger models. It has a four cylinder 1099cc engine of 67mm bore and 78mm stroke. With the side exhaust valves and overhead inlet valves operated by a single camshaft with splash lubrication provided by a plunger oil pump mounted vertically on the outside of the sump, problems were initially encountered because the very short rockers, so close to the valves often became tangled with the long push rods which projected above the block. These difficulties were overcome only by an alteration to the camshaft layout in order to fit longer rockers, thereby distancing the push rods.

The engine clutch and gearbox are in one unit and bolted to the sump which, unlike most vehicles, is fixed to the car frame, rather than the reverse. As a result the engine can be easily lifted from the fixed sump without lifting tackle or the need for draining.

The leather cone clutch drives through a fabric coupling to the three speed gearbox, and the wheels, three stud Sankey artillery, are very strong, light and easily cleaned.

The brakes on the 11.1, however, are not particularly efficient, relying on a cast iron shoe which acts directly on the rear drum with no removable brake linings. An emergency stop at 20mph using both handbrake and footbrake together brings the car to a halt in about ten feet In today's traffic. Steve somehow manages admirably!

When the 11.1 made its appearance it was called the 'Business Man's Pleasure Car'. Because of its round front and back, it also became the first vehicle to be known as 'The Beetle'. The price was £135 and came as a two-seater coupé, with a four-seater available in 1914. It had a wheelbase of 7' 6" and weighed around 9 cwt. The body was constructed from tinned sheet steel bolted to an angle iron and steel frame similar to Gunn's earlier cars which had raced at Brooklands in 1909 and one of which had won the 1910 Moscow-St Petersburg Reliability Trial. Unfortunately, none of these earlier cars is believed to have survived, although some of those sold to Russia after the Moscow run may still be hiding somewhere.

Steve still uses his car enthusiastically and regularly and he did the round trip from Dorset to Oxford for the 1992 Lagonda AGM.

An 11.1 won gold at the 1920 London to Land's End trial.

TA 6980 11.9 Tourer 1923

The 11.9, like this one of Bob Henson's, was the next Light Car from the Wilbur Gunn stable, and several improvements had been made: The steering became geared instead of direct and the engine was enlarged to 69 × 95mm (1420cc) and now had a separate block and aluminium crankcase. The brakes were better too, with bigger drums, each having four shoes fitted inside. By 1922 the selling price had increased to £395, and the wheelbase to 9 feet. But there was still trouble with the rockers and solid forged rockers were used pivoting on hardened pins. There was still no rocker cover. The radiator was different; it was flat squarish honeycombed, as opposed to the very rounded vertical tube construction of the 11.1.

The 11.9 continued the success of its predecessor in the London to Land's End Trial gaining two golds and two silvers from four cars entered in a field of 82 in 1922.

Finally, lighting was very rudimentary. For example, the owner of this car before Bob had it from new, and loved to go dancing in Exeter. But even in those days the local police insisted that parking lights were used and he therefore installed paraffin gas lamps to save the battery.

Note how the rounded rear of the 11.1 has been squared up and a dickey seat added on this model.

PE 7073 12/24 Tourer 1925

The 12/24, like this one belonging to Jim Bailey, was the last of the Light Cars, it has the same bore of 69mm and stroke of 95mm as the 11.9, but there was a big difference: the fitting of a rocker cover and automatic lubrication to the rocker gear.

Also, the leather cone clutch was replaced with a single plate one, and, in 1925, front wheel brakes were introduced. Finally, the radiator was made bigger and more rectangularly upright though it retains the honeycombed construction.

The 12/24 was heavier than its predecessors and its increased instrumentation and levels of comfort showed the way for future generations of Lagondas. Surviving examples, like surviving 11.1s and 11.9s are rare, but Jim's appears to be enjoying life in rural Suffolk.

KO 6393 14/60 Saloon

Peter Jones owns this very elegant 14/60 Saloon. The rear luggage rack on this model is very rare, and can also be put to other uses as you can see from these photos taken at a Lagonda AGM.

YV 1621 14/60
Semi-Sports 1928

Dr Caudle's 14/60 was the only
family car at one time, but as
traffic built up the gearing became
more and more difficult to cope
with. There is a big difference
between second and third, third
being almost like top gear, and
fourth like overdrive. Not
surprisingly, these factors ,
together with the crash gear box
can make driving in traffic
extremely wearing!

Being from 1928, this is one of
the last 14/60s and everything is
original apart from the two spot
lights at the front and fact that the
side scuttle is not quite angled
enough.

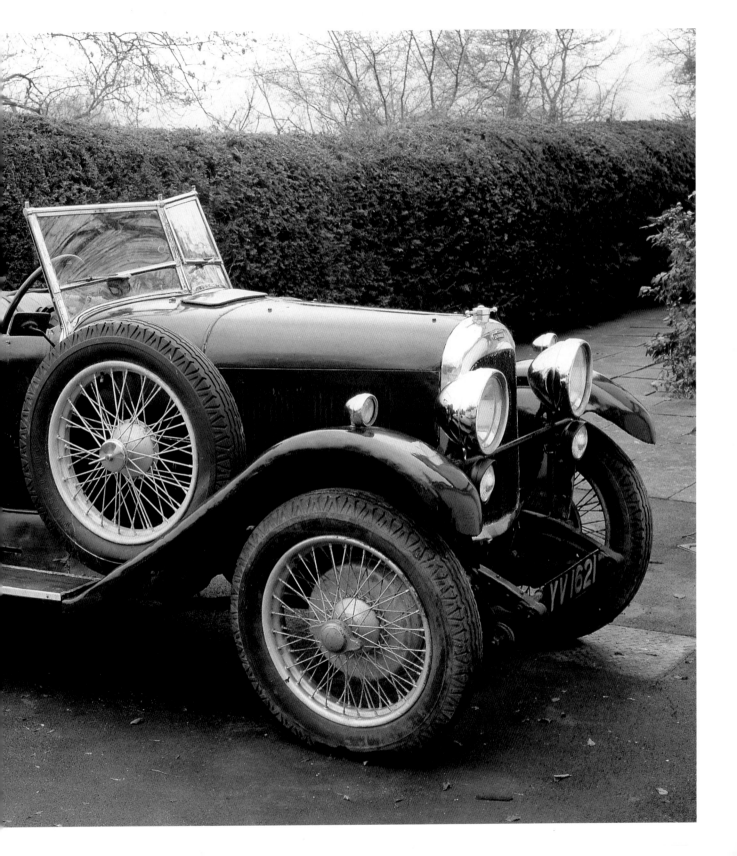

SR 6714 14/60 Semi-Sports 1927

Graham Thomas's 14/60 was at one time left to rot in a field. Fortunately, in 1972, she was rescued by an Edinburgh man from the Dundee chicken farmer who had neglected her, and was restored. (The owner before the farmer was Arbroath's Sydney Burnett who bought the car new in 1928. She remained in his family until 1958.) After the renovations she passed through a number of dealers' hands until Graham acquired her in 1987. Since then, he has rebuilt both the engine and gearbox.

The body is a touring one, and though there was a wider Tourer available, that did not have the Semi-Sports description.

Maroon bodied 14/60 1926/7

John Brown's body is definitely not mouldering here but it is waiting for a new heart. As John Brown, the owner, works abroad so much, he hasn't yet had time to restore his 14/60 Tourer. Still, by the look of that immaculate paintwork, when he does get the chance, the results should be well worth waiting for.

2 litre High chassis and Low chassis

These cars of a 10' wheelbase used the same Davidson and Masters 1954cc engine as the 14/60. However, because of the feeling that the High chassis cars had a more 'authentic' 2 litre feel, soon after their introduction, the 14/60 was phased out.

In 1928 the 2 litre high chassis driven by D'Erlanger and Hawkes finished 11th at Le Mans, despite having a cracked frame and no front brakes for most of the race. The lessons learned there led to the launching of the Low chassis the following year. Several changes were made. The main one was that whereas the High chassis's front brake rods were attached to the underside of the axle, those of the Low chassis passed through it allowing the car to hug the road more safely. Then the Low chassis model was also provided with cycle wings at the front which turned with the steering, unlike the fixed Speed Model wings of its predecessor. Moreover, the brakes, adjustable by a lever under the bonnet were now on all four wheels, with the hand brake operating separate shoes on the back ones. Finally, for ease of servicing, the grease nipples were placed on either side of the car, three on the near side, five on the off.

In 1930 the Low chassis was joined by a supercharged 2 litre model, with a longer bonnet to cater for the blower fitted vertically in front of the engine. Fortunately for Lagonda, space was available for the supercharger on the same shaft as the dynamo which was driven directly from the crankshaft, the dynamo then being mounted in front of the blower. The supercharged cars were given a stronger, more balanced crankshaft and a heavier rear axle to accommodate the extra power. There was, however, a problem; the six right angle bends of the inlet passages meant that the 2 litre engines were already prone to overheating problems. Now, with the introduction of the blower, this tendency was magnified, leading to a certain unreliability as well as soaring fuel bills. The cars did go fast, but, even so, many people removed the blowers.

The last model in the 2 litre range was the Continental. This still had the 1954cc engine with four in-line twin cam overhead valves and five main bearings; a single dry plate clutch with four forward gears, one reverse and a no synchromesh crash gearbox. It still had a single 1.25" SU carburettor. What was different though, was the elegant backwardly slanting radiator which gave the car a very streamlined appearance. New too, the 18" wheels delivering lower gears.

This picture, taken on a pleasantly sunny day at the 1992 AGM, shows clearly the height difference between the Low chassis car (left) and the High chassis (right). Note too the cycle wings of the former as opposed to the latter's fixed ones, and the different sizes of radiator

It's interesting to note in passing that most cars of the vintage period had a different pedal layout from modern cars. The accelerator was in the centre between the clutch and the brake, which made it easier to use the brake and accelerator in unison (heeling and toeing) – very useful when dealing with a crash gearbox. The other complication, meanwhile, for the driver of the High chassis was the close proximity of gear lever to headlamp dipper.

Above
The Gardner brothers' 1927 2 litre High chassis Speed Model was originally a saloon which they have rebuilt as a four seater Tourer. The hood and frame have yet to be finished, but as they point out the car is only really used in fine weather these days

Right
Alec Downie's 2 litre High chassis 1928 Tourer is a very tidy example of the model. No wonder he looks so happy behind the wheel. The car has the standard Tourer body with two doors on the passenger side but none on the driver's side. A clear case of legover and drive! As you can see, the fabric-covered body has no skirt to cover the chassis rail

Above

Colin Mallett's 1927 2 litre High chassis Tourer. This very nice black example looks just right with suitably mellowed stonework behind

Right

Robert Harris's 1927 2 litre High chassis Speed Model, undergoing restoration. There are many cars like this about, hidden in garages waiting for the final touches. This one has a bit further to go on the upholstery and paintwork yet, but mechanically it is fine. Note the headlamp dipper to the right of the driver, with the large round knob to the right of the driver

Jim and Jan Bradshaw's 1929 2 litre High chassis factory-built Team Car replica. Sadly none of the original Team Cars is known to have survived, so this rep is probably the closest it's now possible to get. A beautifully kept and maintained example. The driver's side door is interesting here – it has an aluminium covering and is more cutaway than on the standard car, so as to give the racers a bit more elbow room. Also, the rear wings have a very pronounced 'lip' which clears away any water lurking near the back wheels and so creates enormous amounts of spray. Not very nice if you're following the car in a race! For competition, the original Team cars would have been stripped down (no running boards, mudguards and so on) to reduce their weight

Left
*Mr. Nicholls' 1932 2 litre Low chassis Drophead Coupé has a rare body by Carlton.
The graceful lines at the back provide some very useful luggage space*

Above
*Tim Wadsworth's 1931 2 litre Low chassis Tourer. To overcome the lack of luggage
space on the T2 body, Tim has bolted on a boot – not particularly attractive but useful
when the car is used regularly. Otherwise, the body has a lovely original feel to it*

Above
Jeff Leeks has solved the luggage space problem by means of a rack bolted to the side
of the spare wheel. Handy for carrying gear for 'le pique-nique'. He has also left up
the side screens to the hood for a more wind-free journey in this 2 Litre Low chassis
Tourer from 1931

Right
Terry Weatherley's 2 litre Low chassis is fitted with the standard Tourer body which is
skirted and covers the chassis rail. It still has no driver's door but there is a driver's side
rear passenger door, and two more on the nearside, as on the High chassis car

Colin Bugler's 1931 2 litre Low chassis almost looks stripped for racing with its
unskirted body and lack of running boards

Above

Mr and Mrs Evans's 1930 2 litre Low chassis Tourer has an interesting history. The very light special body is believed to have been built for sand racing. Note the racing straps on the bonnet and the absence of both a skirt for the chassis rail and of a passenger door. The car was driven by H. J. Gould in the 1000 mile run to Torquay in 1932, and also entered for the first RAC run to Monte Carlo. Its sister car, Peter Sowle's GF 1954, is now supercharged. Some people might recognise the familiar face of car fancier Bill Lake in the background

Right

Bill Anderson has restored his 1932 2 litre Low chassis Tourer in an attractive two-tone blue – the original colour was primrose. The car retains, however, the very unusual rear end treatment, with a small boot behind the back seat, reached from inside the vehicle. The spare wheel is fixed to the left hand side of the bonnet, leaving space at the back for a luggage rack

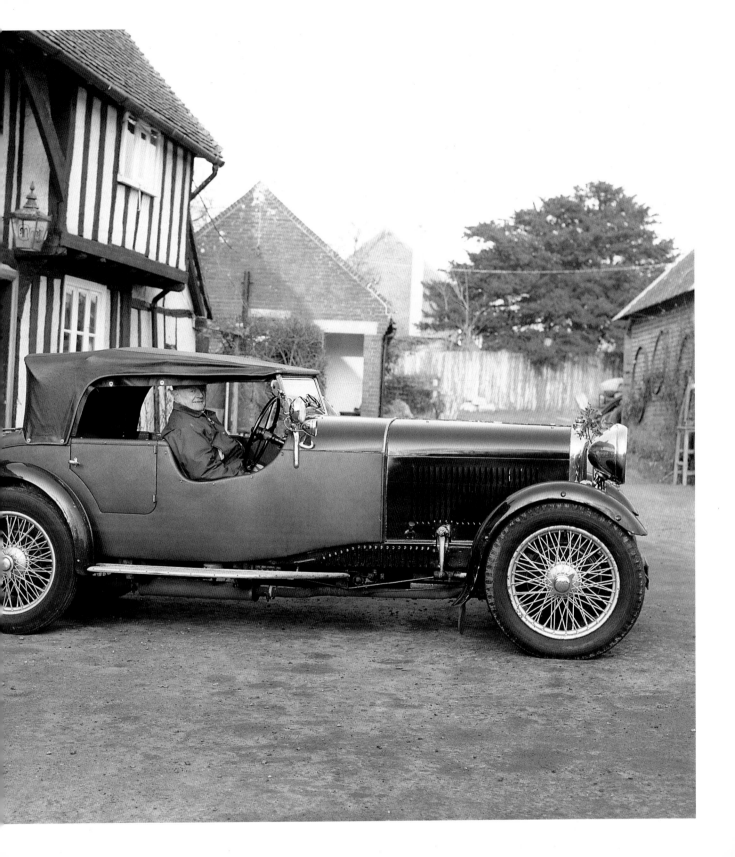

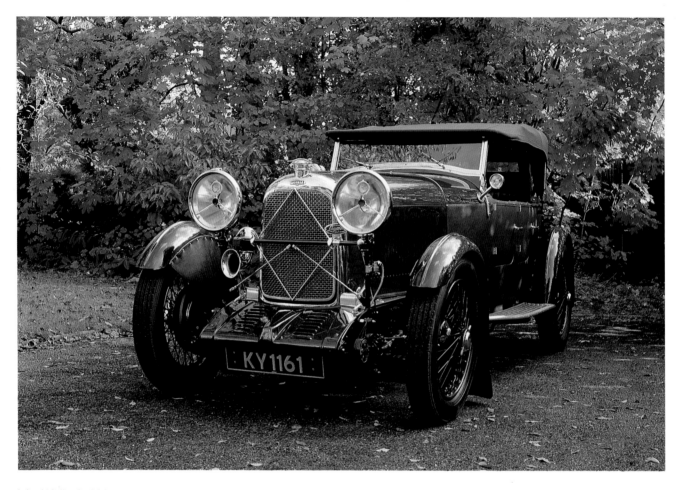

John Walker's 1931 Low chassis T2 Tourer shows off the elegant lines of the 2 litre Lagonda at their best. The car duly came first in its Class A heat of the Benson and Hedges Concours at Knebworth House in 1990, going on to win the final at York race course later that year

The owner of this 1932 2 litre Low chassis, PN 8750 has used it regularly between April and October for 35 years. The car is original as from new and apart from servicing has not been touched since

Above

John Brown's 2 litre Low chassis Speed Model also has an unconventional rear end, but this time the spare wheel has been placed at the back. The car's a two-seater with just the one door on the passenger side

Right

Peter Sowle's 1930 2 litre Low chassis, reg. no GF1954 (yes the same figure as its engine size in cc) has a fascinating past. She belonged at one time to Henry Coates, a very well-known Lagonda Club member who frequently wrote of his exploits, making the car pretty famous too! When Coates had bought her in 1941 she was unblown. He added a Zoller supercharger which apparently transformed the car's performance and smoothness. Yet by the time Peter acquired GF1954 she was unblown again, after a complete rebuild in 1965. The previous owner had been John Cope from Sevenoaks who had put on only 4,850 miles in the nineteen years. High days and holidays I presume! Fortunately though, the blower drive was still installed, and Peter set about having another blower made, a Cozette replica this time. When I photographed the car, it was just about to be fitted, and Peter later told me that after a few initial teething problems GF1954 was again running fast and blown, the only problem being that petrol consumption had increased from 25/6 mpg to 16/18mpg

Bobby Barnes's 2 litre Low chassis supercharged is a T3 bodied car. Fairly rare, this body incorporates a boot of very useful dimensions and a built-in toolbox in the base. The car still has the original Zoller blower and a lower radiator to give more cooling capacity to the supercharger

Another John Walker Lagonda, this time 1931 2 litre Low chassis supercharged one. When John started to research the history of the car, Alec Downie, a fellow Lagonda club member, lent him a scrapbook which had been kept by an enthusiastic schoolboy Lagonda fan. John found the car in there by the registration number and that the first owner had been one W. A. Cuthbert who ran a garage and specialised in tuning sports cars. More research unearthed an article in Country Life *on Cuthbert, an article which mentioned his daughter. John then traced her, and there, hanging on her front room wall was a picture of a Lagonda stripped for racing, without number plates but with a distinctive radiator cap which John immediately recognised. More history emerged: W. A. Cuthbert had come second in the Norfolk Mountain race at the 1932 Brooklands Easter meet and third in the Sprint handicap at the same circuit on Whit Monday. Also, Major Jack Rycroft, who purchased the car from Mike Hawthorne's father in 1935, had raced her at Poole Speed Trials in 1936 and Brooklands JCC in 1937*

These pages and overleaf
Dave Willoughby's 2 litre Low chassis 1931 supercharged car is absolutely immaculate and frequently picks up a rosette as best car in class at shows. Not only beautifully restored, but also pleasantly colourful

The 1932 2 litre Continental with its swept-back radiator and all-steel body, is thought by many to be the best looking Lagonda of them all. Made only between April and July 1932, the car's production run is thought to be 23. Fortunately, most have survived, including this one belonging to Clive Dalton. At the time, a new Continental cost £625 (roughly £16000 nowadays). Clive bought his in 1959 for £130 when the general appearance was tatty. However, after an engine and front axle rebuild and a bit of cleaning up the car went on several long journeys (including to Switzerland in 1961), covered 40, 000 miles and encountered no problems. Then in December 1963, she was taken off the road and restoration started in earnest. It finished in August 1987 – could this be a longest-ever restoration record? The wait looks well worth it though, with the car gleaming again in bright green and chrome

The 16/65 3 and 3.5 litre cars

In 1926, so the story goes, the then Managing Director of Lagonda, Brigadier General Metcalfe asked Davidson and Masters to design a six cylinder engine for a car to be called the 16/65. The result was of 69mm × 120mm bore and stroke producing 2692cc, with push rod operated overhead valves.

The chassis of the 16/65 and the early 3 litre cars had a 10" 9' wheelbase and although bigger than that of the 2 litre, were very similar in construction. The 16/65 was not particularly successful, however, and in 1928 its engine was bored out to 2931cc with 72mm bore and 120mm stroke, and later to 3181cc (75mm × 120mm). The 3 litre was born.

Both engines had seven bearing crankshafts, and were now fitted with twin SU carburettors. At first, 3 litre cars had the same Speed Model fixed wings as the 2 litre High chassis, but later had cycle ones. Lagonda meanwhile, claimed that its great flexibility gave the 3 litre, in top gear, 5 mph and a maximum of 80 mph. In fact with that sort of tractable power, it was possible for a driver to get by on only two gears, first and top, though to get the most from the car, all the gears had to be used. At that point, it became one of the most exciting cars of the period.

Brakes were as for the 2 litre, (four wheel with separate shoes for the handbrake and a wheel under the bonnet for adjustment), but there was a bigger, sturdier gearbox. And in 1932 the winged Lagonda radiator badge made its first appearance. It was to remain thereafter.

The same year the 3 litre Selector Special with a Maybach gearbox was also introduced. This provided twelve gears, split into eight forward and four reverse, ratios controlled by two levers mounted on top of the steering column. The driver could pre-select a gear, which was engaged when he momentarily released the accelerator pedal. The Selector Special came in two chassis sizes, long and short, and had the 2931cc engine.

The final statement of the six cylinder 16/65 engine was the 3.5 litre introduced in 1934. Bored out to 80mm × 120mm producing 3619cc, it had a shorter chassis with a wheelbase of 10' 3". It was also about to be eclipsed by the 4.5 litre car.

Geoff Seaton's 1930 car is the 3 litre. Beautifully maintained and original, this is a vehicle that anybody would be delighted to own. (See front cover)

Above
Russell Jenkins's 1932 3 litre is a rare Carlton-bodied Drophead Coupé with dickey. An elegant and stylish car with graceful helmet wings

Right
Barry Jones's 3 litre Low chassis is used regularly around the lanes of Kent, and often seen parked outside Barry's florist shop in Tenterden. In fact so many people come in to make him an offer for the car, that Barry now puts up a prominent sign beside it saying 'Not for Sale'!

Above

Robbie Hewitt's 1932 3 litre T2 Tourer. Known in the family as 'Auntie', she makes a fine run-about for shopping trips

Right

Philip Walker became the fourth owner of this 1930 3 litre Tourer in 1988. At the time, the car had a cracked engine block and looked as Philip puts it 'very tired'. So he set about restoring her former glory, with the help of the Lagonda Club spares department, and the Vintage Coachworks at Hartley Witney. After 2 years renovation the car was entered for the UK regional round competition of the 1991 Benson and Hedges Concours at Syon Park. She duly won Car of the Day and became National Champion, going on to win the International final at Nottingham too – the first time that a pre-war car had won the title. Then, having been voted the People's Choice, Philip's car was invited to take part in the final of the Benson and Hedges Master Class against previous champions. To his surprise she won there as well, and was once more the People's Choice

Above

Mr and Mrs. Cooke's 3.5 litre Tourer parked next to their M45, is the fun car of the family. With its light racing style cycle wings and lack of running boards, this is a bit of a one-off. The M45 looks low and sleek by comparison

Left

A 1933 3 litre here waiting for some attention in Hugo Spowers's garages at Prowess Racing. This car, a three Position Drophead Coupé, is one of the few twelve speed Selector Specials that Lagonda made, using the Maybach doppelschnellgang vacuum operated gearbox. It later went for auction at Brooks, in Munich and was sold for £16,632

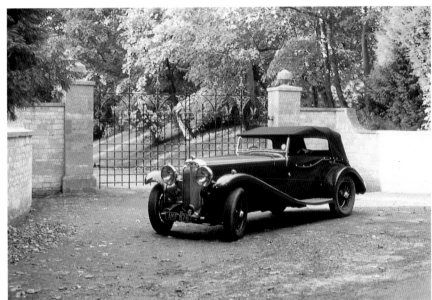

Left

Dave Willoughby's 3.5 litre is here in metamorphosis, with a new wooden frame, and body almost ready for the paint. Experience of Meccano obviously came in handy for assembling the hood frame! And when he's finished, Dave will have trouble deciding which car to go for a spin in. Will it be the 2 litre, 3.5 or Rapier?

Above

Martin Pollard's 1935 3.5 T9-bodied Tourer, has the same fixed wing style as the M45. In October 1937, having had one owner, the car passed into the hands of the Liverpool City Police where she remained until early 1960, being used for advanced driving instruction before the war and skid pan training afterwards. During the war, though, she was parked next to a hut storing oil and petrol and a fire destroyed the hood and frame. Then in 1967, Martin saved her from the scrap yard, having found her behind a row of cottages near Bolton (underneath a tarpaulin). Since then the missing seats, lights, hood and frame have been replaced and the body repainted. Martin uses the car as much as possible in the summer months, including commuting to work. Clearly, the legendary reliability of the Lagonda can survive even modern driving conditions

16/80

In the early 1930s six cylinder cars became *the* thing. So to keep up with the times Lagonda introduced the 16/80, using the same chassis and wheelbase as for their 2 litre four cylinder cars. The 16/80 didn't have a Lagonda designed engine, but a Crossley 2 litre six cylinder unit of 65mm bore and 100mm stroke assembled at Staines and producing 1991cc. There were two SU carburettors and a twin exhaust system. The result was an engine which provided both a docile top gear for town or country, and a rip-roaring sports car performance in the tradition of its predecessors, allowing fast and hard motoring notably free from noise. The brakes were generally considered the best of their day too. Meanwhile, the front passenger and driver now had adjustable bucket seats, and in the back, passengers sat much lower than in previous models, with more protection from the elements and extra legroom either side of the prop shaft. Another innovation was the central folding armrest on the back seat of the open Tourer. In short, a quieter and smoother car which also worked well as a saloon

Peter Heyes's 1933 16/80 Drophead Coupé looks very graceful in primrose, a popular colour for Lagondas at one time. Note too the single panel windscreen with an electric wiper at the top operating two blades

Above

Alan Baker's 1933 T2-bodied 16/80 Tourer has the ENV preselector gearbox, operated by a lever on the right of the driver. There is no clutch but a pedal in the same place that needs to be depressed in the same way. Thus, a simple movement of the lever backwards or forwards and a quick press of the pedal is all that is required to change gear making the process much quicker and easier and eliminating the need for double-clutch gear changes. This ENV gearbox was initially an option, but had became standard by late 1933. Behind the back seat is storage space for the side screens, and beneath it access to the battery. There is also a tool box under the floor panel. The car's rear wings, reminiscent of Bentley, are unusual

Left

Another of Peter Heyes's Lagondas, this time a 1933 T2 bodied Tourer, but unskirted, like the 2 litre High chassis car. It looks very chunky, and has the much stronger cycle wings which were fitted to the 16/80

The M45 and M45 Rapide

Although the 2 and 3 litre cars performed well enough their power to weight ratio was always a problem with much gear changing required to obtain maximum performance. Then, in 1933, Lagonda introduced the M45, using an engine supplied by Wolverhampton-based firm Henry Meadows. It was a six cylinder monobloc of 88.5mm bore and 120.6mm stroke producing 4453cc and had twin SU carburetters. At last Lagondas had real power, and the M45 was the largest sports car made in England at that time. Based on the 3 litre 10' 9" wheelbase chassis, it had semi-elliptic springs in conjunction with André or Hartford Telecontrols and a pair of ordinary André or Hartford shock absorbers front and rear. The Telecontrols had knurled knobs which projected through the floorboards of the car and could be adjusted even while driving. Bigger brake drums, with vacuum-servo assistance, were also fitted, and there was a Meadows all-enclosed clutch. Initially a Lagonda 3 litre gearbox was installed, but this was soon replaced by one of Meadows own. Top speed was now approaching the magic 100mph (approximately 95mph was claimed for the M45). This was finally achieved when in 1934, the M45 Rapide (101mph) made its appearance.

The M45R was based on the shorter 3.5 litre chassis with a 10' 3" wheelbase strengthened at the front to accommodate the larger engine. It had an alloy crankcase, with heavier connecting rods and larger diameter crankshaft bearings. The M45's compression ratio of 6 to 1 was upped to 7 to 1. It was the combination of a beefed up engine with a smaller, lighter chassis which resulted in a quicker machine. At first the Rapide had the same Meadows gearbox as the standard M45, though with a free wheel fitted at the rear, supposedly to ease gear changing. This, however, was replaced after a year by the G.9 gearbox (later to appear on the LG45s of 1936) which had synchromesh on third and top. The brakes of the M45R were Girling, and it had Girling-Luvax hydraulic shock absorbers. The André Telecontrols, adjustable by the driver from inside the car, were retained from the standard model.

Douglas Brown's M45 Tourer, built in 1935, is a very attractive shade of blue. It has been on several trips abroad and when I photographed it, it had just returned from a Lagonda Club jaunt of about 2000 miles. Apparently the French loved it and were quite surprised to find it was English, perhaps because of the colour. Driving an M45, it's not difficult to realise the car's enormous appeal – the distinctive roar from the Meadows engine and that lovely long bonnet in front, whose reflection is picked up in the two big chromed headlights. It all makes for a truly great driving experience, and with the smell of sea breezes all around, an unforgettable one

Above
Philip Erhardt's 1934 M45 has a very attractive body built by Freestone and Webb
and is a Drophead Coupé. From every angle this car looks graceful and sporty, but this
view probably shows off the fine lines at their best

Above right
Seeing Mr and Mrs. Cooke's long, lean and low 1934 M45 Tourer, its not easy to
understand why the Lagonda 4.5 litre was in big demand as a true sports car of its
time. Easy too to imagine Bertie Wooster behind the wheel!

Right
This M45 T5-bodied 1934 Tourer took part in the 1936 Monte Carlo Rally with the
celebrated T. C. Mann behind the wheel. She was placed 60th. One of the few 'one
family' cars still in existence, she is now looked after by Mann's son, Richard

Above

Mike Pilgrim's 1933 M45 saloon has an ST34 body. Note the pillarless but still rigid construction between the doors – an unusual feature of some saloons, and a convenient one too. A very elegant family vehicle this, with a large boot space, and of course that 4.5 litre sports car engine!

Right

This M45 is waiting to have a burn round the track at Silverstone at the Norwich Union 1992 RAC Classic. Not far removed from the all-conquering M45 Team Cars of the mid thirties. This too has the classic lines of the true English sports car of the era

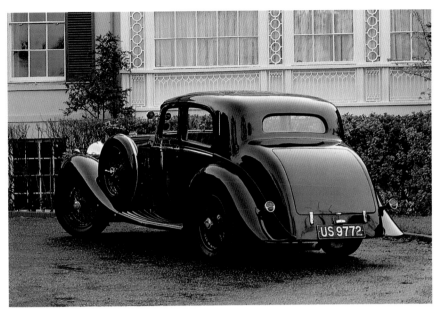

Anthony Dady's 1934 M45 Rapide saloon has a unique aluminium body built by Gurney Nutting. She was displayed on the Lagonda stand at the 1934 Olympia Motor Show, but was probably sold at the Scottish equivalent as she was first registered in Glasgow in 1935. Not much of the car's early history is known, but in the 60s she's believed to have had at least three American owners. The car returned home in 1986 and Anthony bought her the following year

Robbie Hewitt's M45 Rapides – registration numbers BPK 201 and BPK 203 – are both legendary Team Cars. They were prepared and entered for the 1934 Ulster Tourist Trophy race, by Fox and Nicholls, at that time Lagonda's Main Agents. Brian Lewis drove BPK201 and had a well-publicised tussle with Eddy Hall in the 4½ Bentley. Hall eventually got the better of the fight and finished second with Lewis fourth. Meanwhile, BPK 203, driven by Cobb came in eighth. Considering this was their first competition appearance, both cars put in highly commendable performances. The following year, Fox and Nicholls again entered BPK 201 for the Ulster TT on the Ards circuit, this time with the previous years' winner, Charles Dodson behind the wheel. He finished eighth, and another Fox and Nicholls car BPK 202 was seventh. (The story continues overleaf)

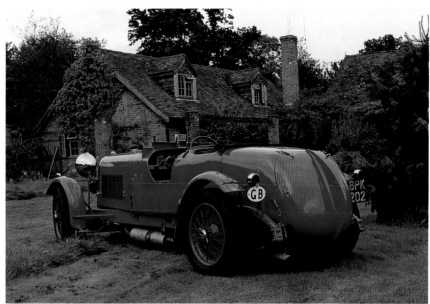

BPK 202 is the most famous of the three Fox and Nicholls prepared M45 Team Cars, and ensured Lagonda a place in history when John Hindmarsh and Louis Fontes drove her to victory in the 1935 Le Mans. In a field of 58, she averaged 77.85 mph, holding off a powerful challenge from Alfa Romeo in particular, on her way to glory. This was the first English win on the Sarthe circuit since the Bentley's (Old No. One) in 1930, and was not repeated until the Jaguar success of 1951. The previous year Hindmarsh had driven BPK 202 to fifth place in the Ulster TT. And in 1935 he took the Le Mans winner to the Ards circuit again, but this time could only manage seventh. BPK 202 now belongs to the Het National Automobielmuseum, Netherlandsz, but is still being raced. When you bear in mind the substantial achievements of BPKs 201, 202, and 203, it's astonishing to think they were not all that different from the standard production M45Rs. In fact, perhaps the only variation lay in the attempt to keep the weight down to a minimum – the normal open Tourers being around 33cwt, the Fox and Nicholls cars nearer 28cwt

Above

An M45 and a 3 litre squaring up, showing the sleekness of the newer car. Note too the 3 litre's larger sump, helping to distinguish it from the slightly smaller, but otherwise very similar 2 litre

Left

Peter Whenman's 1935 M45 TT replica has a 3.5/4.5 engine and is based on the TT and Le Mans Rapides of the 1934/35 period. Another gleaming example of the contemporary coachbuilders art

The Rapier

In 1933 alongside the big M45, Lagonda introduced the smaller Rapier designed by Tim Ashcroft. This had an 8' 4" chassis, and a four cylinder twin overhead camshaft engine of 62.5mm × 90mm bore and stroke producing 1104cc. It had two SU carburetters. The block and head were cast in Chromidium iron, with a very large and strong crankshaft running in three bearings and allowing up to 6000 rpm – at that time unheard of in a production car. Fitted as standard was an ENV pre-selector gearbox providing four forward gears, and operated by a similar lever to the 16/80. The brakes were the latest design from Girling, with large 13" drums and combined great efficiency with a nice lightness of operation. The Rapier was offered as a chassis-only car, bodywork being undertaken by other well known coachbuilders of the day, such as Abbott and Eagle. This enabled customers to choose from many personalised styles.

However, Lagonda sales had always been very seasonal, and when in the spring of 1935, despite the publicity generated by the Le Mans win, they failed to increase after the winter, cash flow problems duly arose. Eventually the receiver was called in. Rolls-Royce were obviously interested, as Lagonda was a main competitor, but in the end a young solicitor called Alan Good beat them to it, paying £67,000 plus £4,000 for the stores. At the time seven different models were made at Staines (Rapier, 2 litre, 3 litre, 16/80, 3.5 litre, M45 and M45R) and Good decided to rationalize. He therefore dropped all except the 4.5 litre. In the face of this decision, Ashcroft, financier Neville Brocklebank, and W. H. Oates who had raced Lagondas before World War I, resolved to carry on the manufacture of the Rapier themselves. After raising enough money to buy the stock of parts, they set up an independent company, Rapier Cars Ltd, at the former sales/service depot at Hammersmith. Coventry Climax were chosen to make the engines to Ashcroft's design and with a 1087cc capacity. Ranalah replaced Abbott as the manufacturer of the majority of the bodies. There was a new badge too and the Lagonda name was removed from the rocker cover on the engine.

Unfortunately, Rapier Cars Ltd wound up in 1938 and was finally dissolved in 1943. Ashcroft had hoped to rejuvenate the company after the war, but this was not to be.

Jim Westland's 1935 Lagonda Rapier has a Corinthian body and is a Drophead Coupé. There were only three Rapiers with this body type made, and Jim's is the sole survivor

Above

The Allens's 1934 Lagonda Rapier was originally an Abbott Tourer but was re-built in 1982 with an Eagle two-seater replica. The Eagle body is rarer than the Abbott, which was the usual one, and with its lack of running boards, looks somewhat racier. Note too the cycle type front wings

Right

G. R. Rowe's 1935 Lagonda Rapier, an Abbott Tourer, was once owned by Major W. H. Oates, the Director of Rapier Cars Ltd from 1936 to 1937. The Rapier came with a very nice-looking spring-spoked steering wheel, and both the radiator and filler-cap were of the quick-action lever type. Standard equipment also included knock-off wheels of racing pattern, and an eight gallon petrol tank with a reserve tank of two more, operated by a tap within reach of the driver

Above

Dr. Mark Frazer's 1934 Lagonda Rapier is another Abbott bodied four seater Tourer. Speeds in excess of 80 mph were possible in the Rapier, but this would depend on the customer's choice of gear ratio – three different back axle ratios were offered, giving the enthusiasts plenty of exciting possibilities. The Hartford duplex shock absorbers kept the whole thing down nicely

Left

Peter Cripps's 1933 Rapier, reg. no. BPC44, has a unique position in the car's history, being the prototype. Also, unlike any other Rapier, she has a March Special two/four-seater Sports Tourer body built by Whittingham and Mitchell. The chassis size is different too, with a wheelbase of 7' 6 ¾" instead of the standard 8' 4".
The car was reputedly built in twelve hours on the Sunday before the 1933 Olympia Motor Show at which she made her first appearance on the Lagonda stand with the also new M45. Both models caused quite a stir. The Rapier was shown too at the Scottish Motor Show in November. Then in the 1934 RAC Rally, driven by Lord de Clifford and despite atrocious weather conditions, she finished the 1000 mile road section without loss of marks. After this the car became the personal transport of her designer, Tim Ashcroft. Peter Cripps has owned her now for over 35 years

This 1935 Eccles Rapier is owned by Alex McCall. The car has many Brooklands and hill-climb wins to her credit, and once lapped the outer circuit at Brooklands at 130 mph, proving the robustness of her supercharged Rapier engine. The main problem involved in turning a sports car into a single seater racer is the centrally placed prop shaft and steering gear. Rather than having a body built over these and everything made very high, as on the ERA, the Eccles car has taken the easier solution. She has retained the driver and mechanicals where they were, and offsets the body by modifying the passenger side, producing a road-hugging and attractive alternative

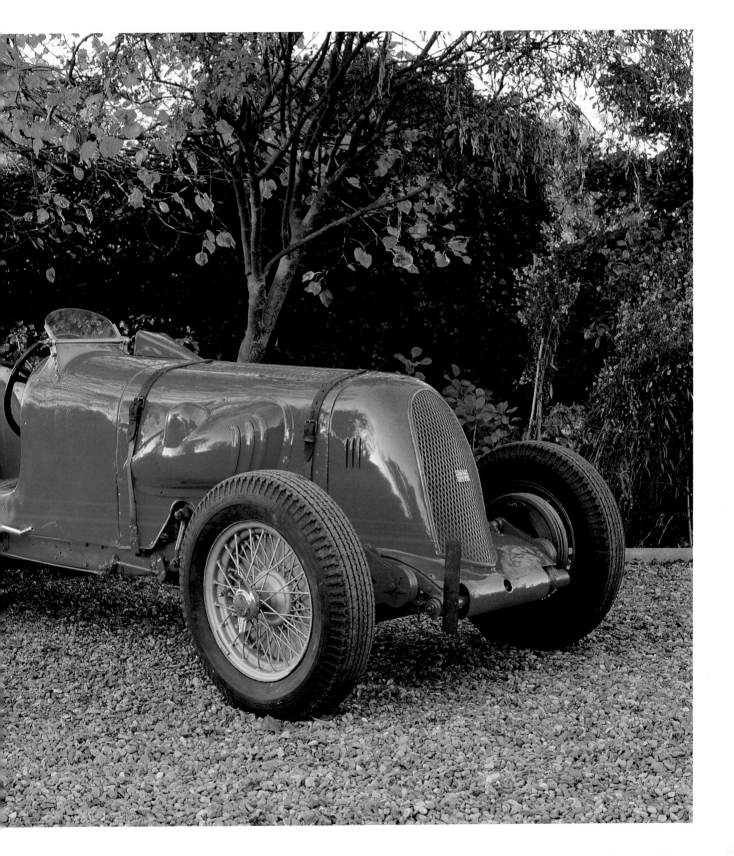

Above

Dave Willoughby on his 1934 supercharged Lagonda Rapier, has built his own single seater body and place it over the prop shaft. This entails strengthening the floor panels and the seating arrangements, all of which adds weight

Right

When Paul Nickalls acquired this 1934 Lagonda Rapier, she had, he says, a 'horrible' 1950s 2+2 body which he removed and replaced with an Eagle replica in 1975/6. He also installed 1½ twin SU carburettors for racing. This is a very rapid car (as the writer can testify!) and Paul makes the most of the incredibly high revving engine. It has won several Trophies, including the VSCC Ladies (1976), the Lagonda Car Club (also 1976), the Baily (1978) and the Ashcroft (1979)

Despite the demise of Rapier Cars Ltd in 1943, a few Rapiers were built after the war
– from pre-war parts by private enthusiasts. This two-seater Derrington Special, for
example, was made in 1951 and is now owned by A. J. Skipper. It's supercharged with
an original Centric blower and 4.6:1 straight cut rear axle. A close ratio ENV gearbox
is also fitted but with the lever on the dashboard instead of being floor mounted

Mike Pilgrim's 1936 Rapier is a Ranalah bodied Drophead Coupé, and a very original car. It was one of the first Rapiers made after the split from Lagonda, and as the radiator had already been drilled to take the Lagonda badge, the new Rapier one doesn't fit properly and looks too low. The Lagonda name has also been filed off the rocker cover

W. O. Bentley's Involvement

In 1935, after 31 years as Technical Director of Lagonda, Alf Cranmer retired. He was replaced by Walter Owen Bentley (known to history as W. O.). By this time the company had been renamed LG Motors, and all of its former models, except the 4.5 litre had been discarded; moreover, although the new cars retained the 4.5 litre engine and the M45 chassis of 10' 9" (later 11' 3"), there was now a trend towards more comfortable driving. W. O.'s initial priorities were therefore to soften the suspension (which he did by means of longer road springs and Luvax dampers and without affecting the renowned Lagonda road-holding), and generally to quieten and refine the engine. The result was a car which, after a facelift by Frank Feeley, combined luxury with sports performance in exactly the way that customers were now demanding. It was given the model name LG45.

LG45s were brought out in batches, known as 'Sanctions', so that any model changes would be reflected in the Sanction number. Thus Sanction One (1935/6) had the same engine as the M45R, but with a lower compression ratio of 6.8 to 1, while Sanction Two (1936), introduced twin Scintilla Vertex magnetos. Then Sanction Three (1936/7) used an improved cross-flow inlet manifold, cast integrally into the head, onto which the carburettors were now bolted directly. It also featured a lightened flywheel; allowing 4000 rpm, and a steel stabilising bar linking the spindles of the rear shock absorbers so as to prevent any oscillation at the back. Sanction Four was similar in many ways to Sanction Three, but was actually fitted to a new car, the LG6. It produced approximately 130bhp.

At the same time W. O. was also working on a new engine, the V12, which was considered his finest when it appeared in 1937. This was a twelve cylinder of V configuration with 75mm bore and 84.5mm stroke giving 4480cc. Compression ratio was 7 to 1 producing 175bhp and could advance the car smoothly from 7 to 105mph in top gear, with 5000

The Hon. Skeffington's 1937 LG45 Saloon has the standard G.10 gearbox, stronger than the G.9 with synchromesh on second as well as third and top. (A centre change gear lever was an option at the time, so as to encourage sales). The car also has Luvax permanent hydraulic jacks controlled from inside a dummy spare wheel cover on the near side. Its Tecalemit automatic chassis lubrication system was another innovative feature at the time

Above

The Peerless family's LG45 Rapide is from 1937. The model came in only one body type, a four seater Tourer, and is a spectacular looking car from any angle. It was fitted with the Sanction Three engine of 88.5 mm bore and 120.6mm stroke producing 4453cc but had a higher compression ratio than the standard LG45 reputedly giving 150bhp. Top speed was in the region of 105mph. A truly thoroughbred sports model

Right

Alec Downie's 1937 LG45 Saloon is known as The Razor-Edge because of the sharp edges on the roof-line. The body is by Freestone and Webb and incorporates a very large and useful boot space in a graceful but still powerful looking car. The Luvax hydraulic shock absorbers, controllable from the steering wheel centre, are simpler than the Telecontrols of the M45

rpm being possible. There were two SU carburettors on the V12 and four on the V12 Rapide.

Bentley designed three new chassis types for the V12 with 10' 4", 11' 0", and 11' 6" wheelbases – the Rapides were on the lighter, shorter chassis and the larger saloons on the longer ones. Meanwhile, compression on the Rapide was raised to 8.8 to 1 upping its bhp to 225 – which, together with the four SU carbs gave the car a top speed of 110mph.

Above
Another LG45R, this one George Dodd's 1937 Tourer. A more efficient exhaust system was also provided using twin external downpipes to remove unwanted burnt gases and heat

Above right
Colin Bugler's LG45 TT replica, based on the Fox and Nicholls Team Cars for the 1936 Ulster TT, driven by Pat Fairfield (killed at Le Mans in the following year) and Earl Howe. They came fourth and fifth respectively; the needle match was once again against Eddy Hall in the Bentley, who held them off to take second place

Right
Alec Downie's 1938 LG45R Tourer is one of the later models. This is a real head-turner wherever she goes, an absolutely stunning example of a powerful and luxurious sports car. As already mentioned, gearing was higher on the Rapides, for the record the overall gear ratios were 3.31, 4.30, 5.56 and 8.66 to 1, giving speeds of approximately 105, 82, 64, and 41 mph respectively

This car is a Lagonda Legend with a fascinating race history. She's one of the Fox and Nicholls two-seater Team Cars mentioned earlier which were built for the 1936 Le Mans and took part instead in the French GP. EPE 97 was forced from that race but then came 14th in the Ulster TT behind the other Fox and Nicholls entries. Next was the 500 mile race at Brooklands, when the car was driven by Earl Howe and Brian Lewis (later Lord Essenden), averaged 113.02 mph and finished third, beating rivals Bentley. All this despite running with no front wheel brakes and with oversize rear tyres. In 1937 EPE 97 finally made it to Le Mans. Driven by John Hindmarsh (the 1935 winner) and Charles Brackenbury, she retired after thirty laps. The same year she took part again in the TT, held by now at Donington. (The Ards circuit was no longer usable following a bad accident involving spectators, caused by a local driver losing control.) Brackenbury was once more at the wheel, this time joined by Martin. Unfortunately the car lost a wheel on the 96th lap and had to stop. In late 1937 she was back at Brooklands, where, in full touring equipment, with a passenger and driven by Alan Hess, she covered 104.4 miles in the hour. As late as 1952 she was 14th in the Nine Hours race. Present owner Terry Cohn maintains the wonderful patina EPE 97 has acquired over the years, and still races. New numbers are about to go on yet again, here this time for a VSCC meet at Weston-super-Mare

The LG6, like this 1937 Drophead Coupé belonging to Tony Sherwood, was the first Lagonda to show the flowing lines that W. O. Bentley and his team were then bringing to the company's product. Coupled with the completely new chassis, was independent front wheel suspension, using long torsion bars and wishbones at the front, with long, strong semi-elliptic springs plus torsion bar stabiliser at the rear. These rear springs were mounted outside the frame. Also fitted to this new chassis were hydraulic dampers, still with controls on the steering wheel, which allowed the car to cope very effectively with all road and driving conditions. Thus the LG6 was a smooth limo one minute, a corner hugging sports car the next – and all at the flick of a switch. In short, it had probably the best English suspension of its time, Rolls-Royce notwithstanding, and provided more ride comfort than even the Derby Bentleys. It also had a new Lockheed hydraulic braking system, using twin master cylinders, which meant that in case of failure on one set of wheels, there was braking on the other

Above

GPH 299, a completely standard LG6 Drophead Coupé, built in May 1938, once belonged to ex-King Bernhardt of the Netherlands. Now, owned by Knut Schmiedel, she lives in Germany – though this picture was taken when she was in England for some attention at Peter Whenman's. The LG6's chassis was longer than that of the V12 so as to accommodate the old Meadows six cylinder in-line engine

Right

Richard Kelsall's LG6 was once a standard-bodied 1939 car, but is now undergoing transformation into a one-off special two-seater racer. Looking very like a large Eccles Rapier, without the off-set body, this car should go very fast when it's finished, considering the light weight of the new aluminium body. Getting it round the bends might be a problem though!

V12

Peter Gwynn was a well known figure in advertising when he decided to spend more time on his other love, the restoring and maintaining of vintage cars. He therefore set up the Vintage Carriage Company near Lingfield in Surrey with famous BBC racing commentator Murray Walker, and has never looked back since. Although Peter works with all marques, his own car is an early Lagonda V12, which was eventually registered in 1938. She's a Drophead Coupé built on the new short chassis of 10' 4", with the Sanction One engine, and slightly smaller headlights . A family car, it has a lovely original feel, and still wins the occasional award.

At the time of the V12's launch, while some people continued to opt for the LG6, preferring the combination of a well-tried engine and a new chassis, for many the lure of the new car was too strong to resist. Although fairly complicated the V12 is acknowledged as W. O's finest engine and he always regretted not being able to develop its full potential, because of the war. After 1945 he worked instead on a smaller engine mainly because the running costs of the V12 were so high. In fact it could manage only 11-16 mpg, and in traffic this figure was closer to 7 mpg; too greedy; even for the automotive aristocrats

Above

Douglas Brown's 1938 Drophead Coupé, designed by Frank Feeley, again shows off the flowing lines of the new shape. Feeley was a vital member of W. O.'s team, starting his Lagonda work with the LG45 facelift, before going on to the LG6 and V12. His influence on Lagonda was to continue after the War. Note the sportier wire wheels on Douglas's car here

Above right

The matching red edging lines on the tyres and down the side of the body make this car quite an eye catcher. She's J. A. Larch's 1938 V12 Saloon which has come to the 1992 AGM at Studely Priory in Oxfordshire all the way from South Lafayette, Indiana, USA. Yet with those white wall tyres where else could the car be from but America?. Note that there is no front quarter light on this saloon, as there is on the de Ville

Right

Nick Channing's 1939 V12 Tourer is the only Lagonda with this Vanden Plas body. The car, which was originally supplied with a metallic finish, has a disappearing hood so as to preserve the lines, and the spare wheel is in the boot, leaving little luggage room. The engine is a Sanction One, built on the short chassis. Before the war, the car belonged to Lady Mary Grosvenor. Then, after some time in the hands of Bill Lake, she went to America, where she had several owners. Nevertheless, when Nick acquired her in the late 80s, she had only 29,000 miles on the clock, having spent some time laid up. Nick obviously enjoys driving the car, thundering along in the fast lane at every opportunity, and well he might – she's an exciting and beautiful example of the best of the late 30s English Sports Tourer

M. A. Walker's 1939 Lagonda is a V12 Rapide Drophead Coupé. These cars, of which only twenty-two were made, were built on the short chassis for lightness, and their body styling was slightly different, with more emphasis on the wings, front and rear. The determination to keep the size and weight down, meant very limited space in the back for passengers. Just one seat is fitted sideways allowing one (small!) person some room

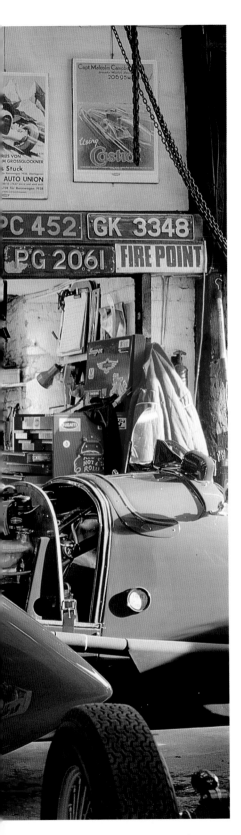

Above

These two replica rear ends show the difference between the muscular lines of the M45Rs of the mid-30s and the more flowing and sleek Le Mans V12 which followed

Left

This V12 Le Mans Replica belongs to Dr. rer. pol. Karl-Wilhelm Putsch, and is here on a visit from Weisbaden in Germany for some problem-sorting on the brakes at Peter Whenman's. Peter can be seen in the background, working on his own two-seater special Rapier, which was about to race at the VSCC Meet at Weston-super-Mare

Right and following pages

Another legend. Phil Erhardt's 1939 V12,
registration number HPL448, was built
by W. O. Bentley and his team in the
Lagonda factory – one of a pair of two-
seaters specially developed for the 1939
Le Mans. As the cars had only just been
set-up for racing and were barely run-in,
by then W. O. was not looking to win,
content that the cars should finish. He
therefore instructed the drivers not to
exceed 5000 rpm. As things turned out,
HPL448, driven by Brackenbury and
Dobson finished third averaging over
86mph. Moreover, the other lightweight
special HPL449 with Lords Selsdon and
Waleran at the wheel, was fourth. It's
now believed that either car could have
won (and that Charles Brackenbury
allegedly took the car to 5600 revs!).
The Lagonda team was not too put out
though, confident as they were of victory
the following year. They were not to
know that war was to come!
Meanwhile on August 7 1939 HPL 448
driven by Charles Brackenbury won
what was to become the last race at
Brooklands, at an average speed of
118.45 mph, and with a fastest
recorded lap of 127.70. Lord Selsdon in
HPL 449 was second, and, in fact,
recorded an even faster lap –
128.03 mph

Jonathan Cook's 1935 M45 Rapide T9 bodied tourer, with a concealed hood when folded, is at last on the road. Bought as 'box of bits', 8 years ago, it has the short chassis of the Rapide, and originally had the usual swept wings of the M45, but due to the cost, and Jonathan wanting to get on the road as soon as possible, cycle wings have been utilised

Specifications

Model	20	30	11.1	11.9 and 12/24	2 litre	3 litre	16/65
Years	*1906–13*	*1911–13*	*1913–19*	*1920–25*	*1926–33*	*1929–33*	*1926–28*
No Cyls	4	6	4	4	4	6	6
Bore	90	90	67	69	72	72/75	65/69
Stroke	120	120	78	95	120	120	120
Capacity	3052	4578	1099	1420	1954	2931/3181	2400/2692
Valves	side	side	oise	oise	ohv	ohv	ohv
CR							
bhp at					60		
... rpm					3500		
Carburation	Poly	Poly	SU/Ze	Ze	Ze	Ze/2Su	Ze
Wheelbase	10'0"	11'8"	7'9"/8'9"	9'0"	10'0"	10'9"	10'9"
Track	4'7"	4'7 1/2"	3'10"	3'10 1/2"	4'6"	4'8"	4'8"
F Suspen			TL	TL	1/2-e	1/2-e	1/2-e
B Suspen			1/4-e	1/4-e	1/2-e	1/2-e	1/2-e
Length	13'6"	15'2"	10'0"/11'4"	12'0"	13'6"	15'1"	15'1"
Width	5'7"	5'7 1/2"	various	various	5'8"	5'8"	5'8"
Weight	16(ch)	22(ch)	12 3/4(ch)	13	25	34	23 1/2(ch)
Top Gear R			3.9	4.4	4.2	4.1	5
Tyre Size	810x90	875x105	700x80	700x80	6.00x19	5.25x21	
Fuel Consum			40			20–21	
Max Speed			37	46	70	83	65

Model	3 litre selector	3 litre	M45	16/80	Rapier	Rapide M45	LG45 (S1)	LG45 (S2)	LG45 (S3)	LG6 (S4)
Years	1932	1931–33	1933	1933	1934	1934	1935–36	1936	1936	1938–39
No Cyls	6	6	6	6	4	6	6	6	6	6
Bore	72	75	88.5	65	62.5	88.5	80		88.5	88.5
Stroke	120	120	120.6	100	90	120.65	120		120.6	120.6
Capacity	2931	3181	4453	1991	1104	4453	3619		4453	4453
Valves	ohv	ohv	ohv	ohv	2ohc	ohv	ohv	ohv	ohv	ohv
CR		6.4	6	6.5	6.9	7	6.6	6.6	7.5	7.5
bhp at		75	108	68	46/60	140	150	140	150	150
... rpm		3800	3100	4500	4500/5000	3100				
Carburation		2SU	2SU	2SU	2SU	2SU			2SU	2SU
Wheelbase	10'9"	10'9"	10'9"	10'0"	7'6 3/4"	10'3"	10'9"	10'9"/11'3"	10'9"/11'3"	10'7"
Track	5'8"	4'9 3/4"	4'9 3/4"	4'8"	4'0"	4'10"			4'9 1/2"	5'0"
F Suspen	1/2-e	1/2-e	1/2-e	1/2-e	1/2-e	1/2-e	1/2-e	1/2-e	1/2-e	I Tor
B Suspen	1/2-e	1/2-e	1/2-e	1/2-e	1/2-e	1/2-e	1/2-e	1/2-e	1/2-e	1/2-e
Length	14'11"	14'8"		14'2"	11'6"	14'11"			15'4"	16'6"
Width	5'8"	5'8"		5'6"	4'9 1/2"	5'8"			5'10"	6'0"
Weight		28		22 1/2 (ch)	18 1/4	33			39 1/4	39
Top Gear R		4.1	3.66	4.6	5.25		3.58	3.58	3.58	3.31
Tyre Size	5.50 × 18	6.00 × 19	6.00 × 19	5.50 × 18	4.50 × 19	6.00 × 19	6.00 × 18	6.00 × 18	6.00 × 18	6.50 × 18
0–50		15		13	9.4	12.6		10.3/11.7	10.4	
Fuel Consum			16	20	25.28	15	16		16/16	13/15
Max Speed		82	92	80	75	100.6	96.6		103.6/91	95.7

Overleaf

Peter Sowle's book; (see page 46). Many Lagonda owners keep past details and correspondence about their cars in this way. It enables future owners to trace the history of the car through garage bills, and descriptions of any renovations carried out. Such books also usually contain plenty of helpful advice and lots of useful diagrams

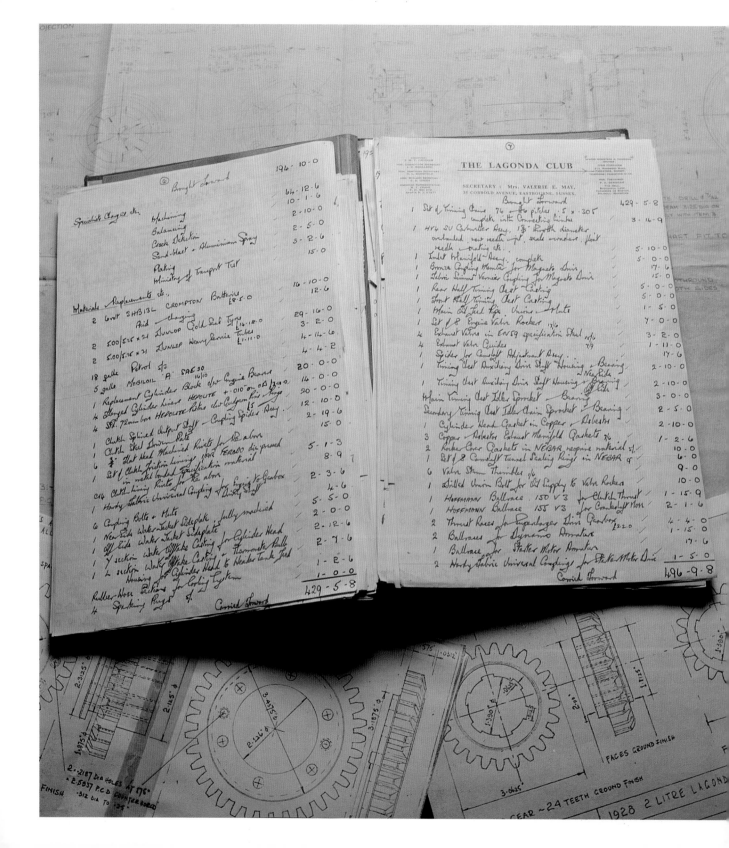